Let Them Have Dominion

Darrell and Pamela Hines

Christian Faith Fellowship Church
Milwaukee, Wisconsin

Unless otherwise indicated, all scriptural quotations are from the *King James Version* of the Bible.

Scripture verses marked AMP are taken from *The Amplified Bible*, Old Testament © 1965, 1987 by the Zondervan Corporation. The Amplified New Testament copyright © 1958, 1987 by The Lockman Foundation. Used by permission.

Let Them Have Dominion
Published by:
Christian Faith Fellowship Church
8605 W. Good Hope Road
Milwaukee, WI 53224
www.christianfaithfellowship.org
ISBN 0-9677535-1-1

Second Printing, March 2003

Copyright © 2000 by Darrell and Pamela Hines
All rights reserved.
Reproduction of text in whole or in part without the express written consent by the author is not permitted and is unlawful according to the 1976 United States Copyright Act.

Cover design by Tom Knauss

Book production by:
Double Blessing Productions
16 1/2 N. Park St. Sapulpa, OK 74066
www.doubleblessing.com
Cover illustration is protected by the 1976 United States Copyright Act.
Copyright © 2000 by Double Blessing Productions

Printed in the United States of America.

Dedication

We would like to dedicate this book to individuals within the ministry who are working side by side with their spouses, and to the fellowship pastors and ministers of Dominion Fellowship Ministries International.

— Darrell and Pamela Hines

Contents

Dedication
Forewords
Introduction

1. God's Original Intent for Mankind 1

2. Serving God Together 29

3. The Role of the Husband 47

4. The Role of the Wife 67

Forewords

The time has come and is long overdue for married couples to minister and preach the gospel side by side. Traditionally many women have labored quietly behind the scenes, faithfully undergirding their husbands as dutiful, passive first ladies and pastors' wives. These women unselfishly suppressed their own spiritual gifts and talents in the name of submission, obedience and tradition.

The time has come for women not only to undergird their husbands but also to stand along side them in the awesome joint anointing that can only flow from a couple united as one in God and the love of Christ.

This book *Let Them Have Dominion*, is filled with not just words but a living testimony of two young people who actually live what they are teaching.

The practical presentation and insight in this book is priceless and desperately needed in the work of the Kingdom to break the chains that only those working together in ministry can unleash.

Reading, understanding and applying the principles found in *Let Them Have Dominion* will strengthen any marriage. Surely the Lord will begin to raise up other great ministries with couples following the great example set forth in this book.

    — *Bishop Ernestine Cleveland Reems*
    Founder/Pastor, Author
    Center of Hope Community Church
    Oakland, California

Strenthening your marriage relationship has never been more important than it is today. We need someone to erase all the erroneous things that we hear and see each day, especially through the media.

God said that everything that He made was good. The institution of marriage was made and ordained by Him, therefore, by definition it is good. Pastors Darrell and Pamela Hines tell us how good this union can be when we do it God's way.

They are experts at directing us on how to achieve balance in our marital lives, especially when couples are working together in ministry. We are familiar with this unique challenge. We have been ministering together now for more than a decade. We have a flow in the spirit as we minister, but it wasn't always like that. We had to learn how to listen to and respect one another. More importantly, we had to learn how to treat each other the way God said that we should (Ephesians 5:21-26;28-30;32,33).

The correlation between the marriage of a man and woman and the marriage of Jesus and the Church is clear. The standard for both of them is the same.

In the following pages, Pastors Hines will show you the good thing that your marriage can become if you will submit yourselves to the will of God.

Read and be blessed.

— Bishop Mack and Brenda Timberlake
Senior Pastors
Christian Faith Center
Creedmoor, North Carolina

Introduction

God has given my husband, Darrell, and I a sensitivity to husbands and wives who both function in ministry. Without any effort on our part, we have become a point of identity for many of them, and we believe it is something that God placed and developed within us.

In the ministry, there are times when God will show you where you are to begin, and He may show you where you will end up — but He doesn't always show you all of the steps in between.

This became the case for us as we stepped out in obedience to God's direction. We have been and continue to be very committed to following the leading of the Holy Spirit in this area.

We accept, embrace, and receive the responsibility that God has given us to bless husbands and wives who function in ministry together.

— *Pamela M. Hines*

Pamela and I had a desire to please God and to fulfill His plan for our lives. We realized that God and His direction for our lives in this area would increase as we sought Him. We knew that the revelation and understanding we needed would never come if we didn't seek for it.

We acknowledged Matthew 5:6: "...they which do hunger and thirst after righteousness...shall be filled" and Matthew 7:7, which tells us to seek and we shall find. Therefore, we understood that there are certain things in God that we had to initiate or we would never find them.

When Pamela and I began to walk into this arena of a husband-and-wife ministry team, that was the point at which revelation of the scriptures began to open clearly to us.

Our purpose for writing this book is to give you an insight into the call of God that is on our lives and the lives of many other married couples within the Body of Christ.

— *Darrell L. Hines*

Chapter 1
God's Original Intent for Mankind

And God said, Let us make man in our image, after our likeness, and *let them have dominion* over the fish of the sea, and over the fowl of the air, and over the cattle, and over all the earth, and over every creeping thing that creepeth upon the earth.

So God created man in his own image, in the image of God created he him; male and female created he them.

Genesis 1:26,27

Many within the Body of Christ don't understand the concept of husbands and wives ministering together. They think it is a new concept, but it is not new in scripture. Neither is it new within the Body of Christ.

It is because of the way we have been taught down through the years that Christians have been slow in embracing what God has called husbands and wives to do in ministry.

When God created mankind, He made both male and female. Sometimes the Book of Genesis can be confusing. People think it records two different creation stories, one in chapter 1 and the other in chapter 2, but the writer is actually recording the same account.

In the first chapter we learn *what* God did, and in the next chapter we learn *how* He did it.

Genesis 1 shows us that when God made "man," He made one man but two *representations*, one male and the other female.

What God literally did was take the female out of the male, and when He did, He made sure that a male would never struggle with being a female, because He took the entire female portion out of him and made a separate female. The word "female" in the Hebrew literally means "the opposite of male."

Created Equally for Dominion

Male and female were created equally to have dominion. The word "dominion" means to have influence or control, to rule by superior power. During creation, according to scripture, the only things that were to be dominated were creatures with feathers, fur, hooves, and gills, and things that crept.

In Genesis 1:28, God gave the male and female the same dominating abilities, and He described the creative authority that mankind — both male and female — have equally.

And God blessed them, and God said unto them, Be fruitful and multiply, and replenish the earth, and *subdue it: and have dominion* over the fish of the sea, and over the fowl of the air, and over every living thing that moveth upon the earth.

This verse says that God blessed *them* and said to *them*, so He was talking to both male and female.

The First Husband and Wife

And Adam said, This is now bone of my bones, and flesh of my flesh: she shall be called Woman, because she was taken out of Man.

> **Therefore shall a man leave his father and his mother, and shall cleave unto his wife: and they shall be one flesh.**
> **Genesis 2:23,24**

This is the first recorded account of a male becoming a *husband*, and the female becoming a *wife*. When a female marries, what qualifies her to be a wife is that she has to be a female. You cannot be a wife if you did not start out as a female. And if you did not start out as a male, you can't be a husband.

That destroys the theory that two men can be "husband and wife," or that two women can be "husband and wife." This may seem elementary to some, but in today's society anything goes, and it is important for us to understand God's original order and intent for mankind.

To be a female means you can become a wife. The Hebrew word for wife in this passage is *ishshah*, which is translated woman or wife. The Bible lets us know that, creatively, she is a female, but when she marries, she becomes *ishshah*, a woman or a wife.

God Ordains Marriage

God described and presented the sanctity of marriage, and He ordained it in Genesis.

> **And Adam called his wife's name *Eve*; because she was the *mother* of all living.**
>
> **Unto Adam also and to his wife did the Lord God make coats of skin, and clothed them.**
> **Genesis 3:20,21**

Although this happened after the fall of man, it still shows us something that is pertinent to fully understand God's original intent for a female in the marriage union.

The married female is called *ishshah,* woman or wife, in Genesis 2, but in this scripture Adam calls her Eve, which means Mother. Each word shows a different responsibility or representation of the female.

Submission of the Wife

Every female is not necessarily an Eve. Remember, Eve means Mother. When my wife was created female, and I was created male, we were created equal both naturally and spiritually, but when she became my wife, she submitted her natural equality to me as the Word of God instructs. I also became submitted, but my position within the marriage is one of headship.

The husband is the head of the wife, according to Ephesians 5:23 and First Corinthians 11:3, and Christ is the head of the man. Ephesians 5:21 says, *"Submitting yourselves one to another in the fear of God."*

The New Testament Greek word for "submit" is *hupotasso,* which means to subject to. Paul was not saying that wives were to become slaves, but that they as well as the husbands were to do whatever possible to please one another in the fear of God.

When we get married, we both have an obligation to begin submitting to one another as we submit to the laws of marriage. And the laws governing marriage, according to Ephesians 5:22 and First Peter 3:1-7, instruct the women to submit to their husbands and Ephesians 5:25 instructs the husbands to love their wives.

Submission Is Learned Behavior

Genesis 3:16 says, "...thy desire shall be to thy husband, and he shall rule over thee." Once married, the woman should no longer desire to live as an unmarried woman. She must understand that now her desire is to be a submitted wife who is pleasing to her husband.

A husband shouldn't get upset if his wife doesn't know how to submit, because it is not a created behavior. She was created to have dominion, not to submit. Submission is learned behavior. That is why Titus was instructed by Paul to tell the older women to teach the young women (Titus 2).

The husband must also apply the Word of God to his marriage and his leadership, because if he doesn't lead properly, it can cause his wife to revert back to her unmarried state of mind, and that can cause a great deal of conflict and strife in the marriage.

Dominion and *authority* are two different things. When a husband begins to understand that, he will recognize that even though he has authority or headship over his wife, it is not the same as the dominion he has over demon spirits or the circumstances of life. It's an authority that keeps governmental order in the married household.

Their Name Was Adam

Genesis 5:1,2 reads:

This is the book of the generations of Adam. In the day that God created man, in the likeness of God made he him;

Male and female created he them; **and blessed them, and called their name Adam, in the day when they were created.**

When God created Adam, He created male and female and he called and considered them both to be Adam. But Adam the male is responsible for calling his wife Eve. Even though every female is not an Eve, in God's eyes every female is Adam and was created and expected to walk in dominion.

When we read scriptures concerning the female, we find that if she is not a wife, a male does not have authority over her. (We are referring to males other than a female's father.)

The only thing that qualifies a man to have authority or headship over a woman is for her to be his wife. If this is not the case, a female is not under any obligation to submit to his authority or headship, because she is equal to him as it relates to ruling and reigning in life.

But as it relates to the married woman, she also has the same spiritual dominion and authority the man has, but according to Ephesians 5:22, she has to submit to the headship of her husband, and she must do so as unto God.

Ephesians 5:22-24 says:

Wives, submit yourselves unto your own husbands, as unto the Lord.

For the husband is the head of the wife even as Christ is the head of the church; and he is the saviour of the body.

Therefore as the church is subject unto Christ, so let the wives be to their own husbands, in every thing.

Learning Submission

How will a wife learn to submit to her husband? Let's look at Titus 2:3-5.

The aged women likewise, that they be in behaviour as becometh holiness, not false accusers, not given to much wine, teachers of good things;

That they may teach the young women to be sober, to love their husbands, to love their children,

To be discreet, chaste, keepers at home, good, obedient to their own husbands, that the word of God be not blasphemed.

One translation of the latter half of verse 5 says, "that the word of God not fall and be non-productive."

Why would older women need to teach young women how to love their husbands and their children? Because loving and submitting have to be learned. And if the older women fail to teach the younger women, we will eventually have generations of young women who don't know how to care for their families and their homes and the result will be that God's Word will be unproductive in their lives.

I thank God for the older women within the Body of Christ. They have experienced many things during their lifetimes, and they know and understand the importance of submission and obedience to one's husband.

The Struggle To Obey

Many have ignored the words "obedient" or "obey" in scripture, but a wife should obey as an act of her willingness to obey the Word of God and to please her husband. (Don't misunderstand us. We are in no way inferring that a woman should do anything that violates the Word of God in order to please her husband, because God's law is the highest law.)

This is one reason that there are so many problems with married couples in the church. Many women don't want to hear this. They think that when they accept Jesus, their marriage will automatically work, but that is not the case. Each person has areas that they must develop — the wife submitting and obeying and the husband loving as Christ loves.

A wife is still a created being who has authority over her own life. In marriage, this can cause great conflict. Some married women say to their husbands, "I know what I need! I know what's best for me. I know what I'm supposed to do, and you can't tell me what to do. I've got my own mind!" If they don't stop this and learn biblical submission, their attitude could destroy their marriage.

The Bible instructs the older women to teach young women because in most cases, they absorb something entirely different from the world.

Men must learn to understand and love their wives like Christ loved the Church, because if they don't submit to God's Word, they, too, will automatically duplicate the ways of the world.

Listening to Wrong Advice

Many of us have been listening to the wrong things. We have been listening to Uncle Wilbert and Aunt Susie Mae.

Uncle Wilbert teaches, "Young man, let me tell you something: Your wife must do as you tell her. You are the man in the house. You are the one who brings the money home. You tell her what to do, and don't allow that woman to talk back to you, either!"

Aunt Susie Mae teaches, "Honey, don't trust any man. You can't trust a man, because I tell you, they'll cheat! They'll keep things from you. Don't you be a fool. Put a little money to the side for yourself!"

You will learn things from these people, but the things learned are not scripturally based. Even after we get saved, we allow the laws of our culture or the laws of our heritage to dictate to us what the laws governing our marriage will be.

However, the Bible must become the standard that you both live by, or you will end up acting like the world. You must submit to the Word of God and respond to each other the way the Word of God says, or your different lifestyles will clash.

If a man tries to get a woman to submit the wrong way, resistance will rise up in her. She should never be beaten or pressured into submission.

The Woman's Role in the Past

When I share certain things, people think I am making them up, but there was actually a time in this country when a law existed which stated that a husband could legally hit his wife with a stick! It was called the Tom Thumb Law. The stick couldn't be any thicker than the husband's thumb.

You may not believe me, but women were once regarded like children in this country. They couldn't vote, and they had no say in what happened in governmental affairs. That same kind of foolishness came over into the church.

You may ask, "Didn't Paul say, 'Let the woman keep silent in the church'" (1 Corinthians 14:34)? That's the problem. We think that "every woman" in scripture refers to every female, but it doesn't. Every female isn't a married woman or a wife. Referring back to the Hebrew word *ishshah*, it means woman, both married and unmarried. The casual reader of the Word will think it means all women, but it clearly doesn't. A thorough study of the context will indicate whether it's referring to married or unmarried women.

When you read and study the scriptures, you will find that whenever Paul referred to submission, he was referring to *married women*. When he said that women should keep silent in the church, he was referring to *married women.*

What prompted Paul to even make this statement was the lack of respect married women were showing to their husbands. They, too, would hear the Word of God, but instead of asking questions or making comments at an appropriate time, they would sometimes ask questions out loud in church. In that day, they had little or no education, and Paul advised them to ask their husbands questions at home, because men were better instructed than women in that day.

Paul was saying to these women, "I don't care how saved you are, or how attuned to spiritual things you become, you still have a responsibility to submit to your husband." So in this passage, Paul was not addressing all females; just the married ones.

Philip's Prophetess Daughters

In Acts 21:8,9 we find an evangelist who had four unmarried daughters who prophesied:

And the next day we that were of Paul's company departed, and came unto Caesarea: and we entered into the house of Philip the evangelist, which was one of the seven, and abode with him.

And the same man had four daughters, virgins, which did prophesy.

How would these young unmarried women keep silent while at the same time prophesy? I have never heard of a silent prophet! You can't prophesy with your mouth shut.

So now it seems we have one group of women keeping silent and another group prophesying.

The prophesying virgins had no husbands and were free to do what God had called them to do. Those who were to keep silent were married.

The Unmarried Woman's Liberty

Notice Paul's teaching in First Corinthians 7:33,34:

But he that is married careth for the things that are of the world, how he may please his wife.

There is [a] difference also between a wife and a virgin. The unmarried woman careth for the things of the Lord, that she may be holy both in body and in spirit, but she that is married careth for the things of the world, how she may please her husband.

There is a difference between *a virgin* (a female) and *a wife* (a woman). What is the difference? The unmarried female cares for the things of the Lord, and no man has authority over her life. Legally, no man can tell her what she can and can't be or do for God.

I would like to ask some of the sisters in the Body of Christ who are dating men who illegally exercise authority over them, telling them what they can and cannot do: Is he married to you? If the answer is no, he doesn't have authority over your life. Your concern should be for the things of the Lord.

Your boyfriend shouldn't be allowed to tell you, "You had better be home at 11 o'clock." He isn't your husband, and he shouldn't try to exercise authority over your life without making you his wife. When he says, "I do," *then* he has a legal right to put demands upon your life because he is your husband.

Paul continues in First Corinthians 7:34, "...The unmarried woman cares for the things of the Lord, that she may be holy both in body and in spirit...." She lives holy both in body and in spirit, wholly and completely given to God, with no man having authority over her life.

Life After Marriage

When a believer marries, he or she is saying to God, "I'm married now, and I'm going to treat this woman or this man the way You have instructed me to in Your Word. This is my first commission."

Prior to marriage, you were an unmarried male and female. Don't try to live an unmarried lifestyle once you get married. It disturbs me when individuals get married but continue to act as though they are unmarried.

Man, you have a wife now, and you have specific responsibilities to her. As a husband, you can't run around the country saying, "I'm going to preach, no matter what my wife says!" *It's wrong for you to put more emphasis on your ministry than on your marriage.*

Remember, men, the Bible says that after you are married, you have to think about your earthly responsibilities and how to please your wife.

If you wanted to fast 30 or 40 days when you were unmarried, you could do it. But now that you're married, your spouse needs to be in agreement with you, or you may have to come off that fast.

If you want to be away from home for 13 weeks in a row when you are unmarried, go! But now that you are married, you must take into account that you have a wife, and providing and caring for her is your responsibility.

When you enter into marriage, you must walk by the laws God has established to govern marriage. You can't make up your own laws, and you can't allow

Grandma and Uncle Buster to tell you how to live a married life if their wisdom is not based on the Bible.

Family "Baggage"

My wife, Pamela, and I came from two different backgrounds, so we came into our marriage with two different mind-sets. We both brought "baggage" that we carried over from our families and past experiences.

Pamela, like most of the women in her family, jumped off the marriage ship when the pressures of marriage became too great. My family, on the other hand, did not care *what* you had to go through — you stayed in your marriage.

After we had been married about seven years, our family backgrounds clashed. I was constantly trying to dominate Pamela. Although my father never verbally said that this was the way a husband should act, I learned it as I watched how he treated my mother.

My uncles would never say out loud, "Make your wife do what you tell her to do," but as I watched them when I visited their homes, I saw how they treated their wives, and I began to treat Pamela accordingly.

My domineering attitude, which was handed down from my father and uncles, began to affect my wife so greatly that she couldn't stand the pressure, and we clashed. Yes, we were both Christians, and we loved God, but after seven years, we realized something was wrong and we needed to change.

We loved each other desperately. I was crazy about Pamela, and she was crazy about me. I wanted to be with her, and she wanted to be with me — but something was missing.

Although we were a married couple, we were living under different sets of laws, so we went to the Bible to see what it told us we needed to do as individuals. We wanted to forget all the things we had learned from our families.

We decided, "You get 'Aunt Julie' out of your mind, and I'll get 'Uncle Buster' out of my mind, and we'll wipe the slate clean and start over."

Starting Over

We made a deal with each other that I would treat her the way the Bible instructed, and I was willing to do whatever I had to do to make that happen. Pamela felt the same way. She was willing to do whatever she had to do to make the Word of God active in our marriage. From that moment on, we began to work on ourselves.

You don't need 20 marriage counselors when you have one word from God. Just open the Bible and make up your mind that you are not searching the Word to find what *your spouse* should do; you are searching the Word to find what *you* are supposed to do.

The wonderful thing about depending on the Word of God is that even if your spouse is not initially following the Word, the power of the Word will eventually cause change, provided your spouse has a heart to follow after God.

Galatians 6:7 says, "Be not deceived; God is not mocked: for whatsoever a man soweth, that shall he also reap." If I am sowing love and righteousness to my spouse, sooner or later it has to come back to me, because the Bible is true.

You may be thinking, "Pastor, you just don't know the type of person I'm married to."

My advice to you is, sit down with your spouse and say, "Listen, this Bible will work for anyone, and I'm ready for us to do what it says. If we are going to stay married, we are going to have to commit to the Word of God."

Marriage: Your First Ministry

Both of you must agree on the Word. Your marriage must become your *first* ministry.

You should conduct no revivals until you get your marriage straightened out. At one point I had to turn down some revivals and go home.

It would have been foolish for me to stay and conduct a revival in Kalamazoo when only God knew what was going on in my home. My wife once said, "You were over in Kalamazoo, but you were coming home to a zoo!"

When you obey the Word, you begin to recognize that you are no longer walking in the male-and-female state; now you are walking in the husband-and-wife state, and you must live by the laws that govern marriage.

When this happens, God begins to honor your marriage, because when it is founded on the Word, it is honorable. The husband and wife become one in the eyes of God, because they are walking by the same laws, and it is God's laws that make you one in His eyes.

Spiritual Adultery

As a man of God, you can have only one wife, not two. As I was coming up in ministry, I often heard other preachers say, "I've got two 'wives,' the Church and my physical wife. My first wife is the

Church, because I am married to the Church. My second wife is my physical wife, and she must understand that the Church comes first."

That philosophy is not in the Bible! It is an old, man-made, traditional way of thinking. What does the Bible say concerning the Church's place in the life of men and women of God? It says that the Church is the Bride of Christ.

Think about that! If you are claiming the Church as your wife, and Christ is claiming the Church as His Bride, someone is committing "spiritual adultery" — and it is not Christ, because He has only *one* Bride, but you are claiming to have two.

How would you feel if I came to your home and said, "I've got two wives, your wife and my wife, but I want you to know that your wife comes first"?

You would reply, "Man, if you don't get out of my house, I'll kill you! What is wrong with you? You claim to have a wife, so you'd better go home to her while you still can!"

Despite what tradition may say, your first ministry as a godly man is to your flesh, bone, and blood — your wife. God sees it like that.

The Two-Headed Monster Theory

While I am at it, allow me to kill the "Two-Headed Monster" theory. There is an old saying, "You can't have two heads. Anything with two heads is a monster!"

In one sense, you are wrong. In another sense, you're absolutely correct. When my wife and I were married, we became "one flesh," and we both became the "head" when it concerned our spiritual authority.

We do, however, understand God's governmental order: (1) Christ; (2) the husband; (3) the wife. When my wife submits to me as the head of the marriage union, we become one. We don't have two heads. As long as she is my wife, regardless of what arena we are in, she is submitted to me.

We must be careful not to reject the laws of God, or we will never learn God's spiritual principles; and there are spiritual principles concerning husbands and wives in ministry that some people will never understand because they automatically separate their wives from the ministry.

Genesis 17: God Calls Abraham and Sarah

God told a man named Abram in Genesis 17:4-6:

As for me, behold, my covenant is with thee, and thou shalt be a father of many nations.

Neither shall thy name any more be called Abram, but thy name shall be Abraham; for a father of many nations have I made thee.

And I will make thee exceeding fruitful, and I will make nations of thee, and kings shall come out of thee.

In Genesis 17:15,16 God continued:

As for Sarai thy wife, thou shalt not call her name Sarai, but Sarah shall her name be.

And I will bless her, and give thee a son also of her; yea, I will bless her, and she shall be a mother of nations; kings of people shall be of her.

It's my personal belief that because Abraham and Sarah were one in marriage, it was important to God to speak to Abraham concerning his wife.

Abraham had to understand God's plan for them both, because had he not understood it, he may not have allowed Sarah to be a part of it.

When Abraham obeyed God by changing Sarai's name to Sarah, I believe it released her to become the mother of many nations, including the nation of Israel, just as God had spoken.

The story of Abraham and Sarah illustrates that the husband must continue to listen to what God says concerning his wife. God knows he is married, and He knows that his wife is his helpmeet, because He called and designed her as such.

The Forgotten Helpmeet

For years, men have placed the greater emphasis on *submission*, because they knew the Bible instructs the wife to submit in all things.

God never said He would make the woman submit, but He did say that He would make her a "helpmeet" (Genesis 2:18). Sometimes men don't allow their wives to help them until it is convenient. It's ironic, but a wife can't *stop* helping, even if her husband doesn't want her help, because God made her that way.

A wife becomes frustrated when she desires to help her husband, but he does not give her an opportunity to help. She may even try to force her help on her husband, but then he may become angry with her, feeling she is trying to tell him what to do when, actually, all she wants to do is help him.

So it is important for the husband to realize that the sooner he shows his wife how she can help in any arena, not just the ones he may feel he needs her, his wife will be fulfilled as the helpmeet God made her.

God knows that if the wife is there when the husband is called, and the man doesn't know what to do with his wife within that call, she will begin to fade into obscurity.

That is why you can go to some churches, and you can't find the pastor's wife. You don't know who or where she is, and a year can go by and nothing is said about her. That's because when God was speaking to her husband about his call, he didn't listen to what God was saying to him about his wife.

Unfortunately, in many churches the wife's responsibility within that ministry is defined by the church members. To some members, she is nothing and nobody; she is just the minister's wife.

Gifts in the Church

I know this isn't a popular message, but it is in your Bible that when God spoke to Abraham about his call, He also spoke to him about his wife, Sarah. That is why I can boldly proclaim that my wife pastors *with* me, because when God called me to pastor, He told me that He wanted my wife to stand with me.

He dealt with me about my wife's role even before I read the scriptures relating to Abraham and Sarah. I hadn't heard of anything like this in my life. But if God can tell Abraham to change Sarai's name to Sarah, He can tell me to have my wife pastor with me.

Ephesians 4:11 says that God has set in the Church apostles, prophets, evangelists, pastors, and teachers. Notice it does not say what *gender* they are. It just says He set these gifts in the Church.

If I am a man of God, and God has truly called me, He may not tell me that my wife is to pastor with me. But I can guarantee you that if I do things according to scripture, I will listen for Him to speak to me concerning my wife. And this concern should apply to anyone functioning in any of the fivefold ministries.

You hear men saying things like this to their wives: "You don't have anything to do with this. You don't have a responsibility where the ministry is concerned. You take care of the house — that's all you are called to — and I'll take care of the church."

Who is going to take care of your part of the home if you are taking care of the church? Your wife is caring for you, the home, and the kids — but who is caring for *her*?

If a man can pastor and keep his part of the law God has given him as a husband, surely a woman can be of some service to the kingdom of God and still take care of her home. I am not just referring to her pastoring with her husband; I am referring to her being of some value to the kingdom, whether it is simply encouraging other women in the Body of Christ.

Peter Speaks to Married Women

Peter writes of husbands and wives in First Peter 3:

> **Likewise, ye wives, be in subjection to your own husbands; that if any obey not the word, they also may without the word be won by the conversation of the wives;**
>
> **While they behold your chaste conversation coupled with fear.**
>
> **Whose adorning, let it not be that outward adornment of plaiting the hair, and of wearing of gold, or of putting on of apparel.**
>
> **1 Peter 3:1-3**

This is referring to married women. Remember, no male with the exception of a woman's husband should try to tell women how to dress; the Holy Spirit will have to do that.

But let it be the hidden man of the heart, in that which is not corruptible, even the ornament of a meek and quiet spirit...

Verse 4 doesn't mean a weak and dead spirit; it means the meek and quiet spirit of a woman who is in submission to her husband.

...which is in the sight of God of great price.

When a woman says, "God, I will submit to this man as my husband because You have said to do so, and I will do it meekly and quietly as unto You, Father," her attitude is of great price to God. She yields her own desires and submits herself to her husband because God said to do it.

For after this manner in the old time the holy women also, who trusted in God, adorned themselves, being in subjection unto their own husbands.

Even as Sara obeyed Abraham, calling him lord: whose daughters ye are, as long as ye do well, and are not afraid with any amazement.
1 Peter 3:5,6

Peter Speaks to Married Men

Likewise, ye husbands, dwell with them according to knowledge, giving honour unto the wife, as unto the weaker vessel, and as being heirs together of the grace of life: that your prayers be not hindered.
1 Peter 3:7

If a husband doesn't have this revelation from the scriptures and also by the Holy Spirit, he can miss what God wants to do in the life of his wife.

Not only does God speak to a man about his wife in scripture; He also speaks to the wife through revelation knowledge. It is important for a husband to discern what is in his wife and to get the necessary knowledge about it from God.

For example, your wife may have a gift of discernment operating within her. She can sense trouble coming, but if you are not open to receive anything from her, you may miss a blessing in your life and ministry.

She may see that a "brick" is going to hit you, but your attitude is, "Hush! I'm the man. I know what I'm doing. Listen to me and shut up!"

Your wife may shut her mouth if she is submitted, and she will even pray for you, but she will also let that brick hit you in the head because you stopped her from helping you!

The spiritual gifts a wife possesses before marriage don't cease when she gets married; and as she submits herself to her husband, he has to release her to utilize those gifts.

For example, if she has the ability to spiritually discern things before marriage, she can spiritually discern things after she is married. If she has a spirit of prophecy before marriage, she can still prophesy after marriage.

Peace Follows Obedience

There may be times for some when their husbands, for whatever reason, may demand that the wife no longer operate in the area of ministry she may have been called to.

My advice to women who experience such predicaments is — because God has called us to peace, and the Bible says, "Blessed are the peacemakers" — the wife should obey the request (in some cases, the demand), of her husband while at the same time praying for him that, according to Ephesians 1:18, God will open the eyes of his understanding and deal with his heart concerning the call upon his wife's life.

I can guarantee you that if she walks in the love of God, she will see a miraculous heart change within her husband, because First Corinthians 13:8 says that love never fails!

Hopefully, the husband has the spiritual sensitivity to say, "God, speak to me about what is in my wife so I can be sensitive to the anointing and the call that is on her life."

If the husband loves his wife like Christ loves the Church, he will try to bring out the gifts of God in her. If she senses something, he will listen when she says, "God is showing me something."

I began to realize that my wife saw things through spiritual discernment, but she wasn't trying to tell me what to do. Some women haven't gotten the full revelation of this; they are too busy fighting with their husbands.

They say things that are critical, condemning, and in many instances destructive to their husbands instead of praying for and encouraging them.

Understanding the Principles

Do you see how a couple's relationship can be so mixed up and unbalanced that it becomes difficult for them to work together because they don't understand the spiritual principles concerning marriage?

If a husband understood the principles concerning Abraham's acceptance of God's call on Sarah's life, it would not be so difficult for him to work together with his wife in ministry.

Abraham's mind-set was, "God, You told me that I'm going to be a father and Sarah a mother, and I thank You that great nations and kings will come forth from us."

When I accept what God has said concerning my wife, I can see it by faith and nurture it within her. Then, when I see it coming to pass in her life, I can say with assurance, "Now I know this is of God." Then, instead of being intimidated, I *include* her, because I need the wisdom that God has placed in her.

I am able to say, "Honey, I was going to sign this, but I didn't hear anything from God. What are you getting?" She may reply, "I feel in my heart that God is saying there is something better."

Or she may say, "Be careful when you go around So-and-so's house, because she doesn't have good intentions toward you."

I shouldn't say, "I don't see that. You're just jealous of her. That's the problem: You're jealous of every woman who comes along. She doesn't intend to do anything!"

Then you notice that Sister So-and-so's skirt begins to get shorter and shorter, and her romantic intentions toward you become clearer and clearer. Now you're saying, "Oh, I see it now!" Too late. Your wife saw the problem when Sister So-and-so's skirt was still around her ankles. She knew it would eventually creep up to her backside, but you weren't open to receive her warning.

"They Say"

Husbands should be praying, "God, what is in my wife? Show me her gifts. What have You placed in her spirit that can be a benefit to this marriage, and, if necessary, to our ministry?"

The result will be that God will begin to deal with you concerning her gifts. For example, if your wife has good business sense, but you don't, why are you keeping the checkbook?

"Well, I'm the man. I'm supposed to be in charge of everything." Have you noticed that the checkbook is always unbalanced, and you never have any money in the bank?

"Well, I can't trust her with it. *They say* if you give a woman a charge card, she turns into a capital CHARGE! You know, *they say...*" You shouldn't be led by "they," but by what the Holy Spirit says about your wife. The Word says in Romans 8:14, "For as many as are led by the Spirit of God, they are the sons of God."

I thank God that He dealt with me one day, saying, "Give Pam all the money to handle. If you don't, you are going to stay broke. Because of your heart, you continuously give money away, and you don't think about saving. You don't have good financial sense when it comes to saving money. You loan money to people and tell them they don't need to pay it back. Since you don't have good financial sense, give the money to someone who does."

I said, "Yes, Lord. She's a woman of God, and she will not take advantage of me. She will cherish the opportunity entrusted in her by God, and she will deal wisely with our finances." In this instance, I was dealing with Pamela according to knowledge.

Peter advised in First Peter 3:7:

Likewise, ye husbands, dwell with them according to knowledge, giving honour unto the wife, as unto the weaker vessel, and as being heirs together of the grace of life; that your prayers be not hindered.

Support the "Weaker Vessel"

Being in a place of authority doesn't mean you know everything; it means you are in a position to establish standards, and you must set the standard of righteousness in your home.

Deal with your wife with honor and knowledge. Give honor or support to her as the weaker vessel. That is the established standard. The word "weaker" applies to your wife's physical aspect.

A husband must dwell with his wife in knowledge, honoring her as a weaker vessel while, at the same time, recognizing that both of you are equal heirs of the grace of life.

I cannot deprive my wife of God's grace because she is my wife. She is just as entitled to share the benefits of God's grace as I am. It would be wrong for me to feel that I can have a prayer life but she can't, or that God can talk to me, but He can't say anything to her. We are heirs together. Jesus gave His life for her as much as He did for me.

"That your prayers be not hindered," Peter said. Whose prayers? The prayers of the subject of this passage in First Peter 3 — the husband.

This says to me that when a husband does not deal with his wife according to knowledge, does not honor her as a weaker vessel, and does not recognize that she is an heir of the same grace he is, his prayers become hindered. His ministry becomes stagnant, and his life and ministry are deprived because of the things he could have had if he had released them in his wife.

I am blessed because my wife has a prayer life. I am blessed because she hears from God. And I am not going to let anyone tell me, "Your wife can't pastor. Any two-headed thing is a monster."

The Power of Unity

My wife is submitted to me. I am the head of my household. *But when Pamela stands in the pulpit, I release her to operate in spiritual things.*

Our congregation is not simply submitting to a woman when they submit to her, just as they are not simply submitting to a man when they submit to me. They are submitting to the same Being who lives in us — and that is the Holy Spirit.

The Bible says, "Wisdom is the principal thing; therefore get wisdom; and with all thy getting get understanding" (Proverbs 4:7). If we could understand the power of unity and why Satan fights so hard to destroy unity, we would begin to see why approximately 50 percent of all marriages in this country — including Christian marriages — end in divorce.

Isn't it strange to you that husbands and wives can't work together in their churches? This has always been a big trick of the devil, and if we would only lower our religious guards and tear down our denominational barriers, we could see this fact.

Many couples need a foundation like this, because their marriages are a mess. Often the cause is disputes over each spouse's place in ministry.

They desperately need someone to address the principles that reveal what God's intention is for those who have a genuine call to work together in ministry and, ultimately, in life.

Chapter 2
Serving God Together

When the Lord revealed to me that my wife was to pastor with me, I wasn't trying to start a new thing or invite trouble. I was only endeavoring to obey God. I had not seen a husband and wife pastor together. I had no patterns to follow; there were no notes or books I could look at; and there were no ministries I knew of that I could draw from.

My father pastored a church for many years, but my mother didn't pastor alongside him. Someone once said that this ought to have shown me that it's not supposed to be done.

That is not what watching my parents did to me. It made me aware that there were gifts and ministries in both my father and my mother, but they lacked the understanding of how to operate them properly.

Since I've obeyed God and said yes to His desires for my wife, there has been a smoother flow to our ministry and pastoring.

I am not implying that my parents didn't do a good job. On the contrary, they did a tremendous job with the knowledge they had, but there is an unquestionable flow of grace for my wife and me as we pastor and labor together. My parents are an intricate part of our ministry today, and they don't mind my sharing these things.

Abraham's Revelation for Sarah

When the Lord told me that my wife, Pamela, was to pastor with me, I didn't know of any examples we could follow, so I began to search the scriptures.

We saw in Genesis 15 that God spoke to Abram, telling him He was changing his name to Abraham. He also told him that He was changing Sarai's name to Sarah. Just as God was making Abraham a father of many nations, He was making Sarah a mother of many nations, and He went on to say that kings would come out of them.

God was really giving spiritual responsibility to Sarah and Abraham. Together they would be the father and mother of many nations. Through their example, we recognize that there is something God has placed in the wife as she stands beside her husband to assist him in accomplishing what God has called them to do.

A husband and a wife have the right and the God-given responsibility to learn how to work together. Not every wife will work in ministry with her husband, but we need to encourage those who do work together and allow God to use them without judging them.

Adam and Eve

When we think about husbands and wives working together, we think about our first famous couple, Adam and Eve. We know that together they disobeyed God and were removed from the garden.

Ananias and Sapphira

There is another famous couple in scripture I would like to bring your attention to. They are Ananias and Sapphira, and their story can be found in Acts 5.

But a certain man named Ananias, with Sapphira his wife, sold a possession,

And kept back part of the price, his wife also being privy to it, and brought a certain part, and laid it at the apostles' feet.

But Peter said, Ananias, why hath Satan filled thine heart to lie to the Holy Ghost, and to keep back part of the price of the land?

Whiles it remained, was it not thine own? and after it was sold, was it not in thine own power? why hast thou conceived this thing in thine heart? thou hast not lied unto men, but unto God.

And Ananias hearing these words fell down, and gave up the ghost: and great fear came on all them that heard these things.

And the young men arose, wound him up, and carried him out, and buried him.

And it was about the space of three hours after, when his wife, not knowing what was done, came in.

And Peter answered unto her, Tell me whether ye sold the land for so much? And she said, Yea, for so much.

Then Peter said unto her, How is it that ye have agreed together to tempt the Spirit of the Lord? behold, the feet of them which have buried thy husband are at the door, and shall carry thee out.

Then fell she down straightway at his feet, and yielded up the ghost: and the young men came in, and

found her dead, and carrying her forth, buried her by her husband.

And great fear came upon all the church, and upon as many as heard these things.
Acts 5:1-11

Ananias and Sapphira have been referred to as "the doomed couple," but they used the right principle in working their deception together, and they were together until the very end. They used a good principle but applied it the wrong way.

Ananias and Sapphira have been preached about so much, people have determined, "I'm not going to be like Ananias and Sapphira!" I agree, we don't want to do what they did, but we should operate by the principle of working together that they operated under.

Just because someone may take a tool and use it to their destruction does not mean that the tool doesn't have any use. They were unified in their deception, and they walked in unity until death parted them.

Aquila and Priscilla

There is another couple in scripture, Aquila and Priscilla, that we don't hear too much about, but the Bible says more about them than it does about Ananias and Sapphira.

This couple worked God's principle of a husband and wife working together with the correct hearts, yet you don't hear them preached about, and you don't hear lessons taught on their particular acts of ministry.

I think this is intentionally done, because Satan wants to keep the Body of Christ in disharmony, and he wants to keep us in the dark about the truths found in the Word of God. He wants us to overlook this not so-famous couple.

Their story begins in Acts 18:1-3:

After these things Paul departed from Athens and came to Corinth;

And found a certain Jew named Aquila, born in Pontus, lately come from Italy, with his wife Priscilla; (because that Claudius had commanded all Jews to depart from Rome:) and came unto them.

And because he was of the same craft, he abode with them, and wrought: for by their occupation they were tentmakers.

Paul introduces Aquila in the same verse he names Priscilla. He does not mention Aquila apart from Priscilla. Therefore, the first mention of Aquila in scripture also mentions his wife. We shouldn't look at them as merely a man and a wife; let's look at them the way the apostle Paul did. Verse 3 says that Paul abode with "them," and the couple and Paul were all tentmakers. What does that say to me? It says that Aquila and Priscilla worked together on their secular job. They did the same thing on the same job.

Work With Your Mate?

Society today will tell you, "Man, you don't want to work with your wife. You need to get away from her eight hours a day so you don't have to hear her mouth!" Or, "Honey, you don't want to work with your husband! You won't be able to have private conversations on the phone. While he's at work, you can go shopping."

Society implies that there is something wrong with a husband and wife working together. People say, "I don't know how you can do it. Don't you get tired of being around her at work and at home?" It is a trick of the enemy to make you think you can't work together.

Verse 3 shows that Priscilla and Aquila worked together. Priscilla helped Aquila in the tent-making business. You may ask, "But isn't tent making hard and heavy work?" Yes, it may be. But if you will release your wife and assist her in what you are doing, together you can find a way that will bring success to any endeavor.

If your wife has a sewing business, and you decide to work with her as a team, someone may say, "Isn't that kind of soft work, when all you do is sew hems?"

This is how the world has taught separation in the home to the point that they will make you think you can't work together. But thank God for the example of couples like Aquila and Priscilla.

A Hidden Truth

Satan doesn't want the principle this couple represented to be established in the earth today. I am not implying that God cannot use unmarried persons, because we all know He does. But there is a truth that has been hidden by the enemy regarding husbands and wives working together.

Genesis 5:2 says that both male and female were called "Adam" by God. Adam is the one who called his wife "Eve" in Genesis 3:20.

Satan attacks unity no matter what level it is on. He attacks unity in the Church, so we have divisions, schisms, various denominations, and doctrines of men. We even have church splits, where people cut themselves off from each other, refusing to work together. And we have divisions in the home, because husbands and wives aren't working with the authority they could have if they would only work together.

You and your spouse may not want to work together, but don't condemn another couple if they do. If your desire as a husband is to be away from the home in the work force or even in the ministry, and your wife stays at home or works at a different location, there is nothing wrong with it.

However, it isn't fair for others to point their fingers and say that couples who do work together are missing God.

Working Together in the Ministry

Acts 18 brings more light onto the oneness of Aquila and Priscilla. They not only worked together in a secular setting as tentmakers; they also worked together in the ministry.

> **And a certain Jew named Apollos, born at Alexandria, an eloquent man, and mighty in the scriptures, came to Ephesus.**
>
> **This man was instructed in the way of the Lord; and being fervent in the spirit, he spake and taught diligently the things of the Lord, knowing only the baptism of John.**
>
> **And he began to speak boldly in the synagogue: whom when Aquila and Priscilla had heard, they took him unto them, and expounded unto him the way of God more perfectly.**
>
> **Acts 18:24-26**

Aquila and Priscilla went to church together, and they taught together.

"A woman can't teach. Isn't that what Paul said?"

Yes, that is what he said, but, again, he was talking about married women taking authority over their husbands. If the theory that a woman cannot teach is accurate, why is Priscilla permitted to teach Apollos in this passage? In Acts 18:26, a woman is teaching a man!

Priscilla, with her husband, Aquila, began to teach Apollos things he didn't know about the way of God. This is a wonderful example of a husband and wife ministering together.

A husband may release his wife to assist him as a helpmeet in any arena. He can have her assist him as he teaches, just as he could have her help him make tents or anything else.

Willing Vessels

A preacher once asked one of our members, "Man, how can you go to that church and sit under that woman? How could you allow that woman to teach you anything?"

When you talk about the things of God, gender has nothing to do with God's plan. It has to do with the will of God being manifested in *willing vessels.*

We have been deceived. We have been taught things we haven't checked out scripturally. We have accepted them, and, as a result, things became difficult for women in ministry. It has even reached the point where women condemn other women for preaching!

A woman came into our church one evening and wanted to get up right in the middle of my message and give me a message she claimed she got from God.

She wanted to tell me that God couldn't use a woman to preach. I thank God for the security in our church, because we won't allow anyone to jump up, disrupt the service, and begin to say anything they please.

Our people understand and have been trained that there is a protocol that must be followed when giving an inspired utterance, so they ushered this woman out as she was screaming, "God can't use a woman!"

I thought to myself, "Isn't that crazy? If God can't use a woman to *preach,* how can He legally use a woman to come and *prophesy* to tell me He can't?" Apparently her "god" had gotten his wires crossed.

Twisting Scripture

Some people become upset and offended when they hear that Aquila and Priscilla taught together. They say, "I'll show you the scripture where God can't use a woman." My reply is, "You can't show me that, because it's not in the Bible!"

Often people take certain verses out of context. I once heard a man of God say that you can take any verse out of the Bible and make it say what you want. That is not what I am doing; I am staying in the Word of God to show you the truths that will set many men and women free.

For example, the word "pastor" is not mentioned in the singular form in the New Testament; and it is found only once in the plural. And when the word "pastors" is mentioned, it does not have a gender attached to it.

> **(Now that he ascended, what is it but that he also descended first into the lower parts of the earth?**
>
> **He that descended is the same also that ascended up far above all heavens, that he might fill all things.)**
>
> **And he gave some, apostles; and some, prophets; and some, evangelists; and some, pastors and teachers.**
>
> **Ephesians 4:9-11**

Called vs. Appointed

Jesus — not man — gave gifts to the Body of Christ. There are scriptures that define what the office of a bishop, an elder, or a deacon is supposed to be.

The office of a bishop as we know it in some circles is not a divine call from God, because it is not mentioned with the gifts given in Ephesians 4. A man is *appointed* to the offices of a bishop, an elder, and a deacon.

I preached this message once and received a bomb threat. The man said, "God called me to be a deacon!"

I said, "No, sir, I am sorry, but God 'called' you to be full of the Holy Ghost. You were 'appointed' to the office of deacon, because the office of deacon is not found among the fivefold gifts mentioned in Ephesians 4:11."

Please understand I am not belittling any of the ministry gifts, because they are all important to the functioning of the Body of Christ. However, the ministry offices God sets in the Church are found here in Ephesians 4:11, and there is no gender connected with them.

God is the One who calls, and He is the Giver of the gifts. Therefore, if my wife had the gift of a prophet before we were married, I must be sensitive to God in seeing that gift in her.

If the Bible is right — and we know it is — my wife and I can teach a teacher, a preacher, a learned man, and those who are eloquent in scripture, just as Aquila and Priscilla did.

Sister Phebe

I commend unto you Phebe our sister, which is a servant of the church which is at Cenchrea:

> **That ye receive her in the Lord, as becometh saints, and that ye assist her in whatsoever business she hath need of you: for she hath been a succourer of many, and of myself also.**
>
> **Romans 16:1,2**

I've heard men say, "No woman can stand behind this pulpit. This place is for men only!" But here Paul said to the saints at Rome, "Whatever Phebe needs to do, and whatever she has been called to do — help her make it happen. Assist her in whatever ministry needs she has, because she has been a succourer of many, including me."

What right would the Romans have had to withhold from Phebe because they personally felt that God could not use a woman? Phebe had brought many people into the kingdom of God. She had helped Paul and others, and *Paul said Phebe was to receive the same respect they would have given him!*

Notice that Paul called Aquilla and Priscilla the same thing — his helpers — in Romans 16:3,4:

> **Greet Priscilla and Aquilla my helpers in Christ Jesus:**
>
> **Who have for my life laid down their own necks; unto whom not only I give thanks, but also all the churches of the Gentiles.**

The word "helper" in verse 3 comes from the Greek word *sunregos,* which is defined as helper, worker, or fellow worker. Its root word is *sun,* which means companionship, together, and completeness.

Paul was telling the Roman churches to greet Priscilla and Aquilla, his helpers, as people who were complete, companions to him, and helped complete him in what he was called to be.

This is the same Greek word he used when he gave Timothy a title in Romans 16:21: "Timotheus my workfellow [helper]...."

Literally, what Paul was saying was, "Greet Priscilla and Aquila my *sunregos* and Timothy my *sunregos.*" He used the same title for all three.

Paul Gives Thanks for Workfellows

Some may say, "That's fine, but Paul didn't call Priscilla and Aquilla 'pastor.'"

If you will notice, Paul never called Timothy "pastor," either! He did, however, call these believers fellow helper, worker, co-laborer, workfellow, and companion, all of which are the same word in the Greek.

We need to understand that a husband has the right to choose his wife to work and pastor with him, and no one can prove it wrong by scripture. The only thing that will condemn what I am saying is the traditions and religious doctrines of men.

People may call me henpecked and say, "He has to check with his wife before he can hear from God," simply because I choose to allow my wife to stand with me in ministry.

Let's look again at Romans 16:4: "Who have for my life laid down *their own necks:* unto whom not only I give thanks, but also all the churches of the Gentiles."

Reading this scripture, we see that Priscilla and Aquila both made the same sacrifice in ministry. Paul did not separate Priscilla from Aquila; neither did Aquila exclude or dishonor Priscilla because she was a woman. Paul never made up a special feminine name for Priscilla as helper, either. Paul understood that she and her husband were doing the same work, so he gave them the same title.

Controlled by the Spirit of Tradition

What I am sharing here is not intended to cause controversy, although I am certain this will happen in some religious circles. What I am sharing is intended to reveal the truth, although, unfortunately, many don't want the truth.

They would rather be controlled by the spirit of tradition that says, "If what I believe got me this far, I may be wrong believing it, but I'll die before I change. I know what you are saying sounds right, but that is not what I was brought up believing. I was brought up believing that women must keep quiet in the church."

It is this kind of conditioning that has kept multitudes of women who have a genuine call of God upon their lives in bondage. The gift of God in them has been so crushed that a spiritual imbalance begins to operate in many of them.

When they finally do have an opportunity to say something to people, they feel the need to "sneak in" what God has to say. The result is an appearance of being out of order, simply because they were never given permission to openly express their hearts or were never allowed to be the women of God they were called to be.

Is There Equality in Ministry?

Is there equality in the eyes of God where ministry is concerned? Galatians 3:28 says, "There is neither Jew nor Greek, there is neither bond nor free, *there is neither male nor female:* for ye are all one in Christ Jesus."

My wife and I make the same sacrifices where ministry is concerned that Priscilla and Aquila made. Paul stated that he was not the only person who thanked God for the ministry of Priscilla and Aquila; all the churches among the Gentile nations thanked God for their ministry team.

The churches didn't condemn this godly couple and tell them they were setting a bad example; instead, the churches praised God for them!

Paul also mentioned in Romans 16:5 the church that was in *their* home — not just Aquila's home, but the home of Aquila *and* Priscilla, which again indicates they were working together. If the church was in their home, I believe it is safe to say they were functioning in the office of pastor.

Some denominations today did not forbid women from ministering in the church as part of their founding doctrine. They did not allow the culture of the country to dictate what would go on in their churches.

At one time women could not vote in the United States. I believe this is where this spirit against women's participation originated, and it moved its way into the churches, even though it is not found in scripture.

Staying Sensitive

Remember, in the domestic setting there is a difference between my responsibility and my wife's responsibility. I will love my wife as Christ does the Church, and my wife will always be in submission to me in everything. This is God's divine structure, and it keeps order.

Pamela didn't come to me saying that God had called her to pastor. In fact, I approached her and said, "God is dealing with me about you pastoring with me. Pray about it." When she said yes to it, the anointing was released in her.

Every six or seven months I ask her again, "Do you still sense the anointing to pastor on your life?" I do this because I understand that God could be pulling her into a different direction, and I desire to stay sensitive to that direction. I know my wife, and if she had her way, she would stay home and clean, cook, and take care of our children and me. This is her first love and her first ministry. She is literally in love with taking care of her home, according to Titus 2:3-5:

> **The aged women likewise, that they be in behaviour as becometh holiness, not false accusers, not given to much wine, teachers of good things;**
>
> **That they may teach the young women to be sober, to love their husbands, to love their children,**
>
> **To be discreet, chaste, keepers at home, good, obedient to their own husbands, that the word of God be not blasphemed.**

Women Against Women

It's strange, but when I began to minister along these lines, I could sense uneasiness in the women in the congregation, even though it is the Word of God.

The Lord has shown me that the world has placed a negative emphasis on scriptural principles, causing even women in the Body of Christ to respond negatively to women who desire to care for their families and their homes.

One of the terms commonly used is "male chauvinism," which was created because men abused their God-given authority. Just because some have abused their place of authority does not make caring for your husband, family, and home wrong. The Bible says it is right, and it is.

My wife came to me and told me she wanted to do what the Bible says she should do in caring for me. We honor the order that God has established in the home.

In turn, I told her that I wanted to care for her; I wanted to make sure she has everything she needs; and I wanted to care for her and love her as God told me I should. I told her I wanted her to trust God in me, and that as she submitted to me, I would be all that I could through the power of the Word and the Holy Spirit. This created a desire in her to do more of what God says concerning our home and me.

Our First Responsibilities

Pastoring and the church come second — the responsibilities of ministry are second to our marriage and our home. My first ministry is to fulfill the duties of a husband and a father, and my wife's first ministry is to fulfill the duties of a wife and a mother.

After we discuss our responsibilities to one another, we discuss how we will make ministry happen while keeping our home life first. God then gives us insight.

My wife loves to stay home and cook and clean, but if she is to pastor, there will be times when she will have to be away from the home ministering and/or traveling with me. So what are we going to do?

We came to an agreement. I will not come home asking questions like, "Why isn't the house clean?" That's crazy when I released her to function and operate in ministry.

If your wife has agreed to take a secular job to help with the expenses of the home and you both are working, something is wrong if the husband comes home, looks at his wife, and asks, "Why isn't dinner ready? Why isn't this house clean? What's wrong with you?" She can't do *everything*. You must find a level of agreement.

Then there is the issue of the children. Who will care for them? We asked God to provide what it would take to maintain our home and function in ministry. We had to find someone to come into our home at a wage we could afford to help us with the cleaning, cooking, and care of our children. This insured there would be no slack in our home.

My wife works with me as a pastor, yet she is still my wife and the mother of my children. I never pressure her to produce beyond her ability when she embraces what I have allowed her to do in ministry.

A Message of Unity

The message we are sending out is one of *unity*, not division. When I embrace my wife before our congregation, we are sending out two messages.

The first says that we are a unit, and we will not allow anything or anyone to come between us. There are too many ministers who allow the church to come between them and their spouse.

The second deals with the husbands of women in church who hear another man placing demands on his wife like, "Come to church. Give your money. Travel out of town with the choir." The enemy can cause great confusion from this, making him think that the minister or pastor has more control over his wife than he does.

But when a husband can see my wife standing next to me at all times, it gives him an assurance that I am not after his wife, nor am I interested in his wife.

As a pastor I have had to establish some boundaries, and having my wife as a pastor along with me has greatly helped me. I do not counsel women alone without my wife being present. I am never alone with any woman without my wife being there, and I don't call any woman or check on anyone's wife unless my wife is with me.

This destroys what the devil can use to bring reproach, division, or confusion. It also makes the trust of the men in our congregation much greater, because they know that my interest is solely in the spiritual development of both him and his wife. The result has been many men coming into the kingdom of God.

If more husbands and wives had stood together in ministry — not necessarily always in the pulpit, but together in the eyes of the people — they would not have had to encounter many of the pitfalls they did in ministry; particularly where it concerns women.

I am not beyond reproach — my flesh can fail just like the next guy — but I have set up safeguards that will aid me in fulfilling God's call upon my life without any avoidable pitfalls.

Chapter 3

The Role of the Husband

Unto the woman he [God] said, I will greatly multiply thy sorrow and thy conception; in sorrow thou shalt bring forth children; and thy desire shall be to thy husband, and he shall rule over thee.

Genesis 3:16

After the fall of man, there were certain things we had to cope with that we would never have been subject to prior to the fall. For example, a man didn't have to deal with being a husband *before* the fall the way he did *after* the fall.

Before the fall, governing or ruling over the woman was not the husband's responsibility. There was no sin, and God did not have to prescribe a governmental order for marriage, because His order was established when He proclaimed that mankind — male and female — would have equal dominion.

If you know anything about sin, you know that it is chaotic, it is without order, and it goes against order and government. Because of the disorderly results of sin entering into mankind when they disobeyed God and fell, God had to establish a new order for mankind to live by.

A Selfish Act

After the fall, a woman's desire was to be to her husband, according to Genesis 3:16, and her husband would rule over her. The phrase "rule over" in that verse is powerful, but it has been somewhat misinterpreted and misunderstood by those who thought it meant "to dominate."

I personally believe that marriage can be one of the most *selfish* acts we can perform. As we grow up — particularly in the church — we see individuals of the opposite sex, and we desire to marry based on our physical needs; not necessarily because we love that person.

I am not saying it is wrong to have those desires, but usually they are based on selfish motives. It is rare to hear someone say that they desire to marry because they want to better the other person's life. When most people marry, they seek to find out how they will be benefitted personally by marriage.

The result is that some people search the Word of God and use the laws He has passed down concerning marriage against their spouse so they can gain personal satisfaction from the marriage.

Ruling vs. Dominating

Throughout the centuries, husbands have seen the term "rule over" in scripture, and instead of gaining a thorough understanding of what God was saying, they felt it was more beneficial to dominate their wives, saying, "I'm the man, and you'll do as I say!"

I am not implying that this is the mind-set of every man, but it certainly has been the attitude of many men in previous generations. In today's society, things are quite different due to the Women's Liberation movement. I am not saying it was a godly movement, but it came into existence because women grew weary of being oppressed by men who didn't know or understand the true order of God.

God does not want us to marry for selfish reasons, because a marriage will never work if it is founded solely on selfish reasons and neither spouse tries to change their motives.

The Foundation of Marriage

The foundation of marriage is stated by God in Genesis 2:24: "Therefore shall a man leave his father and his mother, and shall cleave unto his wife: and *they shall be one flesh.*"

Marriage is not solely for your personal benefit, and as long as you are selfish in your marriage, you will never fully embrace your spouse, because you will always be trying to gratify yourself.

God declared to the woman that her husband would have the rule over her. The word "rule" in the Hebrew means to reign and have dominion, but it also means to govern or manage, giving a different shade of meaning to the word, and making "rule over" somewhat easier to accept.

Usually, when people think of the words "rule," "reign," or "dominion," they associate these words with people who are above others or people who oppress. But when you understand the full meaning of the phrase "rule over," you see it means something for which you have responsibility.

So instead of thinking "rule over" means something you dominate or take authority over by suppressing, it is something that you merely have responsibility for.

In this light, let's reread Genesis 3:16: "...thy desire shall be to thy husband, and he shall manage or take responsibility for thee." Anything a person manages, he must take responsibility for.

I once managed a shoe store, and I was responsible for maintaining the schedule so the store had enough staff on hand to meet the needs of the business.

Sometimes employees were upset with me because of their work schedule. However, my first priority and responsibility were the needs of the business, not the employees, because if the store failed, we would have no further need for the employees. I had to learn how to manage the store for it to produce the results the owner desired.

Marriage Maintenance

Many of us own vehicles. I'm not equating marriage or a wife to a vehicle — this is merely an illustration — but if we do not care for our vehicles, like getting the necessary maintenance, they will not perform at their highest level and will fail to serve us properly.

What an individual is responsible for he must learn to manage properly. When it comes to our marriage and our wives, we husbands have a responsibility to bring out and provide the very best we can.

As a husband, you must be responsible to do all you can to manage, govern, rule, and take care of what God has given you. As you do, your wife will desire to allow you to manage, govern, and rule over and within her life. It will be something she longs for, because you are operating under God's law, which is *the law of love*.

Love then causes the marriage to take a new turn. It is not human love as the world portrays it; it is divine love. Divine love, according to First Corinthians 13:5 in *The Amplified Bible,* is not self-seeking.

Forms of Love

There are many forms of love. *Eros* in the Greek is sexual love experienced between a man and a woman. The world has taken this form of love, which God intended to be experienced within the sanctity of marriage, and perverted it. It is from *eros* that we get the word "erotic," which has sinful connotations attached to it. This form of love is usually entirely selfish.

Phileo, the brotherly form of love, and *storges*, the form of love shared between friends, says, "I'll be your friend if you'll be my friend," and both can be selfish.

Then there is *agape* love, the God-kind of love, which says, "I will love you regardless of what you give back to me."

One extension of *agape* is *agapao*, which is a love of the will; something beyond sex or physical desire in marriage. It is a conscious decision to love that says, "I want to love you. You may not have all the things I thought I needed or I was looking for prior to marriage, but by my will I love you. This love is not based on my physical desires for you but the godly desires within me. When the sensual desire wears off, I don't know what will happen with our marriage, so I am making a conscious decision to love you as an act of my will."

This is the kind of love spoken of in Ephesians 5:25, where the apostle Paul said, "Husbands, love your wives, even as Christ also loved the church, and gave himself for it."

The love that Christ has for His Church is not based on anything the Church has done to deserve it. It is *agape* love, God's form of love.

When the Honeymoon's Over

Something in you becomes satisfied when you are able to do things for another person, loving as a conscious choice, not a sensual one.

This is the problem within many marriages. Our choices are sinful and sexual, but when the fire of sensuality has waned and the honeymoon is over, we seem to lose what propelled our love, and then we don't know what to do.

Often this is the point where people discover that they suddenly don't like or even love their spouse any more. Their love was selfish, and now that the self-gratification is over, or they have become bored through the years with their mate, they are no longer motivated to work to have a successful marriage.

To remedy this problem, the Bible tells husbands to love their wives like Christ loves the Church, and to give themselves as Christ did. Christ gave up His own will for the Church, and husbands must be willing to give up being self-centered for the success and development of that which they love — in this case, their wife. This is how Christ loved the Church.

In the Old Testament, the Mosaic Law stated that if a man was not pleased with his wife, he could "put her away" or divorce her (Deuteronomy 24:1).

Jesus came as the fulfillment of the Law, and He stated in the New Testament that a man should not put his wife away for any cause other than adultery

(Matthew 19:3-10). Why? Because He wanted us to operate under a higher law, the law of love *(agape)*.

Hosea's Wife

Let's look at the Old Testament example in Hosea.

> The word of the Lord that came unto Hosea, the son of Beeri, in the days of Uzziah, Jotham, Ahaz, and Hezekiah, kings of Judah, and in the days of Jeroboam, the son of Joash, king of Israel.
>
> The beginning of the word of the Lord by Hosea. And the Lord said to Hosea, Go, take unto thee a wife of whoredoms and children of whoredoms: for the land hath committed great whoredom, departing from the Lord.
>
> So he went and took Gomer the daughter of Diblaim; which conceived, and bare him a son.
>
> And the Lord said unto him, Call his name Jezreel; for yet a little while, and I will avenge the blood of Jezreel upon the house of Jehu, and will cause to cease the kingdom of the house of Israel.
>
> **Hosea 1:1-4**

Some people think that because Hosea is called a *"minor* prophet," his calling was less important than one of the *major* prophets, but that is untrue. God used Hosea greatly, and in this passage He instructed Hosea to marry a prostitute!

I don't think there is a less desirable woman a man could marry than a woman who has given herself to multiple men. Still, God told Hosea to marry a prostitute.

By doing this, God displayed the incredible love He has for His people. Hosea's action ultimately compares the relationship between a husband and a wife with that of Christ and His Church.

God's Unconditional Love

But in this Old Testament passage, God compares the people of Israel with a harlot. Although He is grieved by their behavior, they are still His people — those with whom He has entered into a covenant relationship because *He* loved them, not because *they* loved Him. In fact, they left Him and went whoring after other gods!

Throughout the Old Testament, we see this comparison between God and Israel and a marriage relationship. There are scriptures where God refers to knowing or not knowing His people, and the word "know" in those passages is the same word that is used to describe the intimate relationship between a man and woman.

For example, Genesis 4:1 says, "And Adam *knew* Eve his wife; and she conceived, and bare Cain...." Intimacy is reserved for marital relationships.

God loved Israel, but they rejected Him when they went after other gods. Nevertheless, His love for them never changed. How was this possible? The love God had for Israel was an act of His will for the benefit of Israel, not for God Himself.

I am not implying that a man should allow his wife to go around whoring and then receive her home with open arms. What I am saying is that a husband's love for his wife should never be based on what she can bring to the marriage table.

Selfish Husbands

Some men say, "I want a woman who is good looking and has a good job, so she can help me financially. She's also got to be strong so we can have six children."

Such men go on and on about all the things they want their wife to have and bring into the marriage, neglecting to share what *they* plan to bring into the marriage. Of course, there is nothing wrong with wanting a good-looking wife and having nice things.

My wife has been a tremendous blessing to me, but I must admit that I was drawn to her for selfish reasons. Pamela was very attractive and had many good attributes. After meeting her, I said to myself, "I've got to have that," so I went after her and married her. My selfish motives quickly began to manifest within our marriage.

The first thing I did was to establish rules within our marriage that would benefit *me*. I manipulated our conversations, making sure that when they were over, Pamela knew *my* point of view, even if I never listened to *hers*. I had her doing and saying things that were in *my* best interest, not thinking about whether or not *she* would benefit from them.

Pamela tried to express her needs and desires to me, but I didn't feel they were important, because they weren't what I wanted. I had to change or lose my wife. Thank God for His Word, because through the Word I was able to save my marriage!

Thinking about Hosea and the awesome task God placed before him to marry a prostitute, we realize it had to be an act of his will, because there is no way in the world that most men would seek out a prostitute as a wife.

The True Foundation for Happiness

Many men have based their happiness on what their wives can do for them. As long as they are basing their happiness on this, they will never achieve that happiness, because at some point their wife is not going to be willing to do what they want her to.

There must be another foundation that will cause husbands to stay with their wives, even if the husbands are not getting their way. That foundation is Jesus Christ, the Word of God!

Perhaps this sounds foolish to some, but the Bible says the preaching of the Gospel to those who are lost seems foolish. It doesn't make sense to the world to think of someone else before they think of themselves.

The world system is designed to keep you in a place where you always watch your back and state, "If I don't watch out for myself, who will?" The world system will never encourage you to do things God's way, because the world operates on a natural, low level that always works against God's order.

When you receive Jesus Christ into your life, you won't have to worry about "you." Just cast your concerns on Him, walk in obedience to His Word, and the Bible says He will care for you.

As *The Amplified Bible* shows First Peter 5:7, "Casting the whole of your care — all your anxieties, all your worries, all your concerns, once and for all — on Him; for He cares for you affectionately and cares about you watchfully."

Loving the Bible Way

Pamela and I have been married for more than 20 years, and I am living out what I am sharing with you. I didn't start out this way, but my love for my wife and my enjoyment of being in love with her has turned the tables, and it is now my joy to make my wife happy.

How did this happen? About 13 years ago, I made up my mind that I was going to treat my wife based on the principles found in the Word of God. I made a commitment to my wife and to God that I would not respond to my wife based on how she responded to me.

I told Pamela that I was going to love her the way the Bible says I am to love her; and it would be because I wanted to, not because of anything she would have to do. I told her I wasn't doing it based on what I would receive back from her, but as an act of obedience to God. I told her I would manage and care for her as an act of my will.

I wouldn't take my example from how my father treated my mother, not that he mistreated her. My father loved my mother deeply with all the knowledge he had, and he still does.

However, when I was a child, I remember thinking that the way my father treated my mother was extremely mean and inconsiderate, but his father was a mean individual, and all he had to pattern his life and marriage after was what he saw lived before him.

I remember thinking, "When I grow up, I won't be as mean to my wife as my father was to my mother." I desired to treat my wife nicely.

Mean Spurts

When Pamela and I were first married, I had my mean moments, but for the most part I was kind to her even in my spurts of foolishness.

I said mean things to her like, "Get in there and cook me something!" Or, "You're going to do like I say," "Don't say anything back," "Hush," "I said —

shut up," "Look at me when I'm talking to you," and "Why don't you do what I tell you?"

I had these spurts that I adapted from my father and uncles' examples, but I didn't know any better.

When I share these things with our congregation, they can't believe that I ever talked to Pamela like that. They love Pamela dearly, and I have to ask them not to become angry with me, because this happened many years ago, and I didn't know any better.

When I came to the point where I almost lost my wife, I had to decide that I wanted my marriage to work, and I needed to find out what I needed to do to make it work.

Deciding To Walk in Love

Our emotions are often governed by our will. I can be mad at you and maintain an attitude, or I can *choose* to ignore you. It's an act of my will.

I can walk in love or strife as long as I want to. It's a fleshly, selfish act, but God made us free moral agents, and we have the ability to choose what our actions will be.

No one can *make* me angry; I make a *decision* to be angry. We must learn through the Word of God and the Holy Spirit how to take control of our emotions.

Therefore, *the first step to become a successful husband is to walk in the God-kind of love,* or *agape.* Always remember that you and your wife are heirs *together* of the grace of life. Work together toward a purpose, just as God has ordained and mapped out in the Word of God.

You can't govern your marriage by your own ideas. If you want your marriage to work, you must love your wife just as Christ loved the Church.

If you come home and the house doesn't look the way you would like it to look, love your wife and walk in love with her anyway. Don't love her based upon how much money she brings into the home. Don't love her based on how much she responds when you are in a conversation or how she submits to you.

One thing I have learned about submission is that it is easy for a woman to submit when she feels she is being properly cared for. If you want to have problems with your wife submitting, let her feel like she's not being cared for. I guarantee you, she will have a problem subjecting herself to you!

Ignoring Society's Dictates

Society would say that Hosea was a fool. He married a harlot out of obedience to God, and she returned to her sinful lifestyle after they were married. But Hosea was obeying God. Likewise, your marriage must be something greater than what society dictates it to be.

Society says, "If she's not treating you right, get out. Why pay for someone who is not going to respect you?" But what did Hosea do?

> **Then said the Lord unto me, Go yet, love a woman beloved of her friend, yet an adulteress, according to the love of the Lord toward the children of Israel, who look to other gods, and love flagons of wine.**
>
> **So I bought her to me for fifteen pieces of silver, and for an homer of barley, and an half homer of barley:**
>
> **And I said unto her, Thou shalt abide for me many days; thou shalt not play the harlot, and thou shalt not be for another man; so will I also be for thee.**
>
> **Hosea 3:1-3**

Although Hosea's wife continued to commit adultery, he made a decision to stay with her.

If Christians are confronted with a similar situation, Jesus has given us the right to divorce when the cause is adultery. However, if you decide to stay with your spouse, *there will be grace for you to get through the tough times,* for there are principles taught in the Word of God to help you.

I have found that unbelievers will put up with many things in marriage that some Christians, who are supposed to have the love of God shed abroad in their hearts, won't even consider dealing with.

Some sinners say, "Well, I love her, and I know she's doing me wrong, but I want to be with her," while the Christians may say, "What does the Bible say? Can I get out of this? If so, I'm gone!" People who are ready to leave that quickly don't have their will in line with the Word of God.

Israel proved to God many times — just as Gomer proved to Hosea — that they could not be faithful, but God loved them just the same.

The Basic Instruction to Husbands

You will not find volumes of books recorded in the Bible on how you as a husband are to conduct yourself within your marriage. In fact, you will find more scripture addressed to wives than to husbands. Woman are told how to dress, talk, care for their children, and submit to and honor their husbands.

There are detailed instructions to wives, but the Bible basically tells men to love their wives like Christ loves the Church.

That may seem somewhat unfair until you recognize what loving like Christ loves really entails.

> Love endures long and is patient and kind; love never is envious nor boils over with jealously, is not boastful or vainglorious, does not display itself haughtily.
>
> It is not conceited (arrogant and inflated with pride); it is not rude (unmannerly) and does not act unbecomingly. Love (God's love in us) does not insist on its own rights or its own way, for it is not self-seeking; it is not touchy or fretful or resentful; it takes no account of the evil done to it [pays no attention to a suffered wrong].
>
> It does not rejoice at injustice and urighteousness, but rejoices when right and truth prevail.
>
> Love bears up under anything and everything that comes, is ever ready to believe the best of every person, its hopes are fadeless under all circumstances, and it endures everything [without weakening].
>
> Love never fails [never fades out or becomes obsolete or comes to an end]....
>
> **1 Corinthians 13:4-8 (AMP)**

This kind of love, God's love becomes a foundation in the marriage. He wants us to love each other unconditionally.

Many of us within the Body of Christ know we have not been as faithful to God in our walk as we should have been, yet His abounding grace is still working on our behalf.

We have proven over and over again that we are not as faithful to God as He is to us, and we don't love Him as He loves us. In fact, if Jesus' coming to redeem us had been contingent on our response to Him, He would never have left glory!

> For the husband is the head of the wife, even as Christ is the head of the church: and he is the saviour of the body.
>
> Ephesians 5:23

The Head of the Wife

The word "head" in this verse doesn't simply mean *authority*; it also means *protection*. Of course, the head of anything is the one who is in authority, but let's embrace the entire meaning of this word "head."

Your body depends on your head for care. The head sees, hears, directs, coordinates thoughts, and it is responsible for the body functioning properly.

Christ has said that He loves His Body, and He wants to be responsible for it.

> Husbands, love your wives, even as Christ also loved the Church, and gave himself for it.
>
> Ephesians 5:25

What does the Bible mean when it says Christ gave Himself for the Church? It is not simply referring to the sacrifice He made by giving His life at Calvary. Christ stepped out of His place in glory — His kingship — to become a man. He gave up who He was so we might become who He wanted us to be.

When you understand this, you can see why Hosea was able to walk with Gomer regardless of her faults and her failures. He was loving her as God loved Israel and as Christ loves the Church.

Sowing in Love

Hosea understood that if he continued to sow seeds of righteousness toward her, one day he would reap the harvest.

> **"Be not deceived; God is not mocked: for whatsoever a man soweth, that shall he also reap."**
>
> **Galatians 6:7**

Don't get upset if your wife is giving you hell on earth, and you are giving her nothing but fire and brimstone. When a man exercises godliness in his marriage, it will be difficult for his wife to take unfair advantage of his love if they are both Christians.

Why? Because the same spirit of love you are operating in — the love that caused you to love your wife as an act of your will — is also moving upon her heart and is causing her to desire to submit to that love. Her desire will change when you begin to exercise your godly headship.

Your wife shouldn't have to beg you to get out of bed and get a job. However, if that ambition is not in your heart, and your grandfather, father, and uncle told you to find a woman who can support you, you won't properly care for your wife.

It's important to stay with the Word of God, because when you do, it will expose you to the truth, and the truth will elevate you to another level of consciousness. *You can rise no higher than you have knowledge,* but once knowledge has been imparted to you, you are accountable for that knowledge.

James 4:17 says, "Therefore to him that knoweth to do good, and doeth it not, to him it is sin."

If you don't desire to be a good husband, you shouldn't be reading this book, because you will receive knowledge by reading it, and you will be accountable for that knowledge.

Love That Goes Beyond

Your desire must be to benefit your wife. Your love must go beyond what she will do for you.

If you are unmarried, your attitude should be to find someone whom you can care for and love, a woman you can express your will to love and cover, and to give her a life worth living. She should wake up each morning looking forward to being with you. After Jesus, her first and last thoughts should be on you.

So ought men to love their wives as their own bodies. He that loveth his wife loveth himself.

For no man ever yet hated his own flesh; but nourisheth and cherisheth it, even as the Lord the church:

For we are members of his body, of his flesh, and of his bones.
Ephesians 5:28-30

Notice that verse 28 says that the man who loves his wife loves himself. That is a transition that happens in marriage. *When you marry, your wife becomes an extension of you.* When you care for her, you are caring for *yourself* through her!

After my wife and I were connected in marriage — after we became one flesh — I learned that what I do for Pamela affects my life. We are not separate anymore; we are together — and being together causes what is invested into my wife to come back to me.

When a husband begins to love his wife as Christ loves the Church, that love changes her and causes her to become excellent ground to be invested in. Then her husband can plant seeds of love, affection, and godliness into her life.

You can't stomp your toe and your head not feel it. The husband and wife are one, just as the physical body is one.

A Praying Husband

My responsibility as a husband is to wake up each day in prayer, seeking God's direction for how I am to supply what is necessary for my wife that day. I do not pray first about my ministry, because my *first* ministry is my wife and family. Many ministers want God's direction for the people, but they forget to pray for their own wives!

Our focus as husbands should be to ask God to make us husbands or men who can provide for our wives the things that cause them to be complete. Each day is different, so be careful not to become regimented or "religious" in your attempts to care for your wife.

What happens on those days each month when she is on an emotional trip caused by hormonal changes? The last thing you should do is respond to her the wrong way. Remember, husbands must dwell with their wives according to *knowledge.* Ask God to give you wisdom on how to treat her during those times.

The Spirit of God will assist you in every situation you encounter if you always acknowledge your need for Him in your marriage. Otherwise, you will be limited to depending on your own reasoning, which is usually carnally driven, and you will take offense at her disposition instead of walking her through it according to knowledge.

Your Common Enemy

Never forget that we have an enemy, and it is his greatest joy to bring division between a husband and a wife. So don't be surprised if Satan tries to influence your wife not to conform to the Word of God when you are doing all you can to love her.

Even if you treat your wife as you should, it may seem that the more you do, the less appreciative she becomes. Satan will try to convince you that she is taking advantage of your kindness.

He will put such thoughts in your mind as, "You see, if you were hitting her, she wouldn't be talking to you like that," or "Since you have changed for the better, she won't tell you where she's going or what she's doing."

That's a trick of the enemy, and you must never be ignorant of his devices. If you give heed to the voice of the enemy, he will push you to think that the Word isn't working the way it should. Then your fleshly nature will rise up, and you will be back to square one.

You must be a doer of the Word and cast down thoughts and imaginations, according to Second Corinthians 10:5, that would cause you to do other than what God has said.

Remember, Jesus never retaliated against those who rose against Him, nor did He change His approach toward the people He loved. He understood that there was an ultimate place of victory He would achieve, and nothing hindered Him from loving His Bride, the Church. So should it be with husbands and wives.

Follow what the Word of God teaches about marriage, and before you know it, you'll be a joy in each other's life!

Chapter 4
The Role of the Wife
By Pastor Pamela Hines

I have been married for more than 20 wonderful years, and I desire to share what God, not the world or my past, has placed on my heart regarding marriage.

Sometimes we wives wonder if our ministries have been hindered by our marriage, or we wonder what God has called *us* to do. As a wife, your concern should really be what you have *not* been called to do, because when you are a wife, you *are* in ministry. *Marriage is a ministry all by itself.*

> **Unto the woman he [God] said, I will greatly multiply thy sorrow and thy conception; in sorrow thou shalt bring forth children; and thy desire shall be to thy husband, and he shall rule over thee.**
>
> **Genesis 3:16**

The Bible says that your husband shall rule over you. In an earlier chapter, my husband shared that the word "rule" means to govern, reign, or have dominion over. This means that a wife is no longer able to do what she wants to do. Her will and her desires no longer have first place in her life.

If you are a woman who wants to hold on to your position in first place, it's too late if you are married. Your husband is now your ruler. If you didn't want someone having the say-so in your life, you should have remained unmarried.

I realize this is a strong statement, and many women will have a problem with it, but it's right there in the Word of God. I did not misquote or misinterpret what the Bible says. The fact remains, your husband has the rule over you.

The Bible also says that your desire shall be to your husband. Your longing, yearning, strong attraction, and stretching out after will be toward your husband. After you say "I do," all you long for — all your attractions — should now be toward your husband.

The Submitted Wife

> Wives, submit yourselves unto your own husbands, as unto the Lord.
> **Ephesians 5:22**

The word "submit" means the supported part of a two-person union. You are the support of your husband. Neither of you is superior or inferior. God has made you one flesh, and your husband happens to be the head. Submission is a humbling experience; one that must be learned.

> **The aged women likewise, that they be in behaviour as becometh holiness, not false accusers, not given to much wine, teachers of good things;**
>
> **That they may teach the young women to be sober, to love their husbands, to love their children.**
> **Titus 2:3,4**

Titus said we must learn to love our husbands. When we females were created, we were created with the same ability to approach God as the man. We had the same dominion and creative ability as man. We could speak, and things would obey us just as they obeyed man. We could and can still speak the Word of God concerning our lives and see results.

Jesus Submitted to His Father

But when we women marry, we submit our headship to our husbands. Everything that God has placed within us *as a wife* must be given and brought under our husbands. We must learn to sacrifice.

Jesus submitted everything He had to God. He said, "Father, not my will but thine be done."

Submission is something we do because it is the will of God, not necessarily because it is something we want or desire to do. We do it because it is God's will. When submitting, we do it as unto the Lord.

I believe that had God not said for us to submit to our husbands as unto Him, at least 90 percent of wives would not do it. But God said for us to do it as unto Him, because He knows we love Him, and we desire to please Him. Submitting as unto the Lord insures it will be done.

Submission: A Spiritual Act

When you submit yourself to your husband, you are being spiritual, for *it is a spiritual act to submit*. When you submit, you can assist in the will of God being done in your husband's life.

A wife has an effect on a husband that no other person can match. *When you married your husband, something supernatural happened.* Suddenly you had control over someone's heart, mind, and emotions.

Now you are capable of making someone other than yourself happy. On the other hand, you are capable of giving him all kinds of trouble, too.

You have the ability to upset his entire day. You have the ability to distract him from everything he needs to do. And you have the ability to keep his mind on you 24 hours a day!

Every wife has the same responsibility toward her husband, whether he is born again or not. When God saved you, you became your husband's drawing card for salvation.

The Unsaved Husband

Whether your husband is a drunk, a drug addict, a liar, or a cheat, you are capable of drawing him to God because of your chaste lifestyle, as Peter wrote in First Peter 3:1,2:

Likewise, ye wives, be in subjection to your own husbands; that, if any obey not the word, they also may without the word be won by the conversation [lifestyle] of the wives;

While they behold your chaste conversation coupled with fear.

Your husband's friends may be coming to your house and drinking beer, cursing, lying, and watching unclean things on television. You can be in their midst serving them just as if they were men of God, and your husband's friends will begin to tell your husband things like, "Man, your wife is something else! You'd better hold on to her and act like you want her, because if you don't, I do."

The result will be that your husband will see God in you, and he will desire what you have. Regardless of how he cuts up, continue to treat him as if he were saved.

God doesn't look at a love walk within your marriage any different if your husband isn't saved, because, according to First Corinthians 7:14, the unbelieving husband is sanctified by the believing wife:

> **For the unbelieving husband is sanctified by the wife, and the unbelieving wife is sanctified by the husband: else were your children unclean; but now are they holy.**

Understand, the unsaved husband's spirit man is not born again because his wife is. However, when a believing wife and an unbelieving husband are intimate, God doesn't see it as an unclean union because of the believing wife. God respects the union and considers it sanctified. He is not a marriage wrecker. He will work with you and help you. He will change your husband.

Don't treat your husband like he's a dirty sinner if he's not saved. Don't talk to him in a nagging way. That is not the way to win him. If you nag him, you will push him away from God; but if you will allow your light to shine, God will draw him to Himself, according to Matthew 5:16:

> **Let your light so shine before men, that they may see your good works, and glorify your Father which is in heaven.**

The Law and the Sinner

The laws of marriage do not apply to unsaved persons, because they can't be expected to live the Word of God without the Spirit of God.

You can't expect people who don't know Jesus to walk according to the laws of scripture in any area of their lives. Some persons may try to do it, but God does not expect it of them.

So if you are married and you accept Jesus, but your husband remains unsaved, you must understand that your spouse is not under the law of God's Word.

In First Corinthians 7, you will find what the spiritually legal grounds are for you to remain married to your spouse. If your spouse decides that he or she doesn't want to walk with God, and they don't want you because you have been born again, and they decide to leave, you are not bound to that marriage.

If you share that you have received Jesus, and your spouse doesn't have any objections and is pleased to stay within the marriage, the unsaved spouse will be sanctified by the saved spouse.

While we are on this subject, let me say that we do not in any way agree with a wife's having to do anything her husband may request that violates the Word of God or the wife. If your spouse physically abuses you, we encourage you to seek help and if the abuse persist; we don't believe that God would have you stay in such a marriage.

I know this may be controversial among some denominational people, but no one knows what you are living with at home. Some people will encourage you to stay with a physically abusive husband. *They* are happily married to a believing spouse, but *you* are a prisoner in your own home!

Allow God — not people — to direct decisions concerning your marriage. You can also seek godly counsel, but make sure that it *is* godly.

The Unfulfilled Wife

Most don't like the word "duty," but it is our duty to submit to our husbands and allow them to walk in the call God has placed on them. Any wife who tries to take charge of her husband will be an unfulfilled wife.

Every husband carries the initials H.P. after his name. The Bible considers him the *High Priest* of his home; but if the wife is leading him and dragging him around by the nose, telling him what to do, we call him *Hen Pecked.*

Understand who you really are as a wife. Many of us who said "I do" really *didn't*, but since we said it, it is important for us to know the power we possess as wives.

You can be a bad wife, or you can be a good wife. You can build your house, or you can tear it down. The Bible says in Proverbs 14:1, "Every wise woman buildeth her house: but the foolish plucketh it down with her hands."

If you know anything about constructing a building, it usually requires some skill, and you must have some type of knowledge before you begin.

What Is the Foundation Of Your Marriage?

The first priority of any builder is to insure that the foundation is solid. What is the foundation of your marriage? Is it based on how "Uncle Bubba" treats "Aunt Mary"? Or did you get married on the foundation that you were tired of working?

Did you get married on the foundation that you needed a place to live? Did you get married on the foundation that everyone around you was getting married, and you were getting old, and it was time? Did you get married on the foundation of a one-night stand, and you had a baby, and you refused to let the man go? Did you get married on the foundation of lust because he looked good? Or did you marry on the foundation of pure love?

Regardless of what foundation your marriage is built on — even if it is built on the wrong foundation — it is not too late for God to help you improve it.

As we saw in Proverbs 14:1, wives have the ability to condemn. We read that a foolish woman plucks her house down with her hands. This means we women are able to condemn things we have built.

When we take that power and use it positively, we can tear down the kingdom of Satan that has been built in our homes! But you should never use the ability you have to condemn against your husband. Use it on Satan, for you have the power to tear down everything in your marriage that has been built on an unsecured foundation.

Influential Women: Delilah and Samson

Women are powerful. There is no one on Earth like us! We are "awesome." We have one of the most powerful spirits in the world, and we have a powerful influence.

Samson was one of the strongest men who ever lived, but Delilah exerted an enormous influence over him, even though they were not married.

You can read their story in Judges 16. Armies of the Philistines came against Samson, and once he slew one thousand of them with the jawbone of an ass. Samson also fought and killed wild animals with his bare hands.

Samson often spent the night at Delilah's house. On one occasion, Delilah, who was secretly working for the Philistines, tied Samson up with brand-new braided cords. While he slept, she cried out, "Samson, the Philistines are upon thee!" — and he broke the cords as if they were pieces of thread.

Eventually, Samson told Delilah the secret of his strength, and he was captured by his enemies. All it took was a little woman named Delilah to bring down the strongest man in the world!

Jezebel and Ahab

Jezebel and her reputation are recorded in First Kings 21. One writer describing her said that her husband, King Ahab, was a puppet in her hands.

Jezebel was such a terrible woman, she caused her husband to become one of the most wicked kings who ever existed. She also killed God's prophets and threatened the great prophet Elijah.

Eve and Adam

Eve is another example of an influential woman. She and Adam were kicked out of the Garden of Eden because Adam harkened to the voice of his wife instead of following the voice of his God. You can read their story in the first four chapters of Genesis.

Adam was the leader of the garden; God had given him directions and instructions to keep things in order. But when he listened to Eve, her influence caused him to lose everything God had given them.

As wives we can use our influence in a godly or an ungodly way. We can help our husbands be the men God has called them to be, or we can see to it that they never walk in their call as a husband, minister, or businessman.

Remember, no one has the kind of effect on your husband like you do. If you desire to be a fulfilled married woman, you need to cooperate with God. He ordained marriage; He knows exactly how it is to work; and He knows how you will be fulfilled.

Obeying the Word

When you submit yourself to your husband as unto the Lord, you are pleasing God. When it comes to blessing and helping your spouse, you won't think of your actions as "submission," because the Bible clearly says you are to do to others as you would have them do to you.

For some reason, we don't think of that scripture, or the one that says you will reap what you sow, but those scriptures also apply to our mates. We don't believe we are supposed to let our light shine, or we are supposed to have brotherly love toward our husbands.

We don't believe that the Word applies. We think we can treat our spouses any way we want, and God will accept it, because they belong to us. However, we must realize that the Word of God *does* apply.

You are responsible for how you respond to your husband. Never forget that he belongs to God, and he is a child of God. God holds you accountable for how you treat your husband.

You are to be subject to him in everything, even if he doesn't know what he is doing! You know you could do it better, and you know it might not turn out right the way your husband is doing it, but you are subject to your husband in everything.

As a wife you do have a say in how things should be done, but your husband has the last say. You might want to tell him, "Honey, it's not going to work like that," but, no, let him do it his way. God will show him what is right, because you are going to be praying, "Lord, show him!"

The Perils of Competition

Satan wants husbands and wives to be in competition. He wants a wife to compete with her husband, and once you begin to compete for certain ground in your marriage, you will always find yourself competing. Don't allow this problem to begin in your marriage. You are not in *competition* with your husband; you are in a *relationship* with him.

Your first responsibility is to your husband and his needs. You are supposed to be concerned with his well-being. Trust me — if God has something else for you to do, He will bring it to pass in your life. You don't need to force your way, and you won't have to worry about your ministry, because *your marriage is your ministry,* and anything outside of that is something extra. Your real ministry is to your husband, because God wants it that way.

You should be willing to give up everything to be exactly what God wants you to be. This is not my personal doctrine. God ordained this.

Your husband needs you. Once you realize this, you will want to do God's will concerning your husband even more. Your husband can do nothing successful or lasting without you, even though many men believe otherwise.

The truth is, you are both one, and if your husband does anything without your support, it is almost as if he is doing it as half a person.

The Husband's Counterpart

And the Lord God said, It is not good that the man should be alone; I will make him an help meet for him.

Genesis 2:18

The phrase "help meet" in this verse means to be the counterpart of the man. If your husband tries to reach a goal without you or your support, there is something vital missing in his life.

The Bible says in Proverbs 18:22, "Whoso findeth a wife findeth a good thing, and obtaineth favour of the Lord."

When your husband has your support, God's favor will rest on him in whatever he attempts to do.

When God joins you and your husband together, it is because the man longs for you to be by his side. He wants you there because you were taken out of him. Then, when God joins you together, *you become the part that was missing in his life.*

If a man never marries, that is a different thing. A different set of laws apply to an unmarried person. However, when God joins a man and wife together, the husband begins to feel complete.

Marriage: A Model of the Church

God said it isn't good that man should be alone. He didn't mean only in the physical sense; He meant in the spiritual sense as well.

When you marry and consummate your marriage, spiritual things begin to happen. You begin to think, talk, and act alike. You have someone your emotions are connected to; someone who will be there for you if the whole world begins to fall apart around you.

Marriage is a model of the Church. When a husband adores his wife, others outside the marriage may get sick and tired of hearing all the good things he says about her!

Some will say, "He's always talking about his wife. He must be doing something wrong, because no one talks about his wife that much unless he is trying to cover up something."

Comments like that expose the enemy's influence, because the husband is supposed to act like that in every marriage.

Characteristics of a Good Wife

When you are a good wife, your husband can't wait to come home. When you are a good wife, his entire day could have been terrible; but if he can just make it home, he knows that everything will be all right. He knows that the house is going to be clean, because the Bible instructs the wife to be a keeper of their home.

When you are a good wife, your husband knows he won't have to fall over things after he enters the house. He knows he won't find the kids running around the house in dirty diapers, screaming. He knows he won't find you on the phone, wearing a rag on your head and a big muumuu dress with dirty, rundown house shoes and night cream all over your face.

When you are a good wife, you watch the clock. You may have looked pretty bad all day long, but you know your husband will be home in an hour, so you get it all together. You turn off the television and turn on the answering machine, because your honey is coming home! As wives we should keep our homes clean and always endeavor to look and smell good for our husbands.

Often we think that sexuality isn't spiritual, but, yes, it is. When Solomon spoke of entering into his garden, he wasn't talking about the Bible or the Temple of God. He was talking about the state of innocence Adam and Eve were in, in the Garden of Eden. The Bible says that they were naked, but they were not ashamed.

Sexuality in Marriage

When married individuals are romantic, some think that sexuality is unclean, but it isn't. There is a Hebrew word referring to a wife that is *therapia*, which means that a wife is therapy to her husband. She is a therapist, and she has the ability to straighten out anything that ails him physically.

The Song of Solomon actually reveals Jesus' relationship to the Church, because marriage is a model of the Church. Let's look at this passage from the Song of Solomon.

> **How beautiful are thy feet with shoes, O prince's daughter! the joints of thy thighs are like jewels, the work of the hands of a cunning workman.**
>
> **Song of Solomon 7:1**

Allow me to say that wives should always take extremely good care of their feet. There is nothing wrong with getting a pedicure to keep them soft and beautiful.

> **Thy navel is like a round goblet, which wanteth not liquor; thy belly is like an heap of wheat set about with lilies.**
>
> **Thy two breasts are like two young roes that are twins.**

> Thy neck is as a tower of ivory; thine eyes like the fishpools in Heshbon, by the gate of Bath-ribbim: thy nose is as the tower of Lebanon which looketh toward Damascus.
>
> Thine head upon thee is like Carmel, and the hair of thine head like purple; the king is held in the galleries.
>
> How fair and how pleasant art thou, O love, for delights!
>
> This thy stature is like to a palm tree, and thy breasts to clusters of grapes.
>
> I said, I will go up to the palm tree, I will take hold of the boughs thereof: now also thy breasts shall be as clusters of the vine, and the smell of thy nose like apples;
>
> And the roof of thy mouth like the best wine for my beloved, that goeth down sweetly, causing the lips of those that are asleep to speak.
>
> **Song of Solomon 7:2-9**

May I remind you that Solomon wasn't at the Temple, and this book is just as important as any of the others in the Old and New Testaments.

The Purity of Romance

There should be romance in your marriage. There is nothing wrong with romance, and it is not unclean. For years, the attitude that sex is unclean has been a trick of the enemy to keep married Christians blind to the truth of the purity of romance, thus eliminating oneness from marriage.

Religion and tradition will make you embarrassed and ashamed of what I am sharing. Satan wants love and romance out of your marriage so he can distract you with romance through someone other than your spouse!

Understand that sex within the marriage union is not just an act of responsibility; it was instituted by God to fulfill a man *and* a woman's desire for each other. You can be as creative sexually as the Bible allows you to be.

There is nothing wrong with sitting down to a candlelight dinner with your spouse, and there is nothing wrong with putting on attire that enhances what your spouse desires to see in you.

However, if you insist on walking around the house wearing rollers in your hair and ignoring personal hygiene habits, the enemy will distract your spouse, because you must meet the physical desires of your spouse.

When Romance Leaves

If we would be honest, we would admit that there are a lot of testifying Christians who do not like being married, and they don't enjoy having sex with their husbands. They don't even like their husbands to touch them.

This is because they have allowed the romance to leave their marriages, and they have hidden behind the Bible, claiming that God is not pleased with sex.

The next thing they know, some smooth-talking, fine-walking female has taken an interest in their man on the job, and now the very thing they thought God didn't approve of is being ministered to their husband by another woman — because they failed to read about it in the Song of Solomon!

Make Time for Romance

Most people won't like this, but married couples need to take one day a week — even if it means taking a day off work —and go someplace to be romantic with their spouse.

A husband needs to talk nicely to his wife and tell her sweet things, letting her know that she has the same appeal to him that she had when they were courting. A husband also needs to wear cologne, brush his teeth, and use mouthwash, because nothing is more distracting to romance than bad breath!

A wife needs to wear something sexy and appealing. It's all right to show your physical body to your husband. After all, he is *your* husband.

From time to time, make reservations at your favorite restaurant. Get dressed up and look good for each other. Let your mother or mother-in-law keep the children for the night. Then enjoy each other and do what Solomon suggested.

Strength in Submission

Society will continually dictate the exact opposite of what I am sharing. People will try to make you feel that you don't have a mind of your own because you submit your desires to the things your husband wants to do.

However, the will of God is for you to be subject to your husband, not *inferior*. Being subject to him is a powerful thing. There is so much strength in being submitted, you will never have to worry about yourself when you submit.

Doing the Will of the Father

God will cause your husband to meet every one of your needs. Every desire you have will come through him because you are doing the will of the Father.

God will always look out for you when you do what is right. If you are not being submitted, and you are always trying to usurp your husband's authority, telling him what to do, God will not move on your behalf.

However, if you will humble yourself under the mighty hand of God, in due season God Himself will exalt you. When you humble and submit yourself to your husband, you are doing so as unto God. Then He will place an ornament of grace upon you, for He highly honors your submission, as Peter wrote.

> **Likewise, ye wives, be in subjection to your own husbands; that, if any obey not the word, they also may without the word be won by the conversation of the wives;**
>
> **While they behold your chaste conversation coupled with fear.**
>
> **Whose adorning let it not be that outward adorning of plaiting the hair, and of wearing of gold, or of putting on of apparel;**
>
> **But let it be the hidden man of the heart, in that which is not corruptible, even the ornament of a meek and quiet spirit, which is in the sight of God of great price.**
>
> **1 Peter 3:1-4**

Meek, Not Weak

Notice Peter uses the word *meek*, not *weak*. Anyone can be loud and boisterous, but it takes strength to be meek and not lash out at every circumstance your husband confronts you with.

God thinks it is priceless when He can find a woman who is willing to submit to her husband. He is gratified when a woman stands, looks society and anyone else who may disagree with His way of doing things in the face, and walks in submission to her husband.

As Christian women, we must be very careful not to take on the world's attitude concerning a woman's place in marriage. It should be our earnest endeavor to be examples to the world of what God will do in the life of a woman who will walk according to His ways within her marriage. The world needs to see godly wives who are blessed not only spiritually but naturally and physically as well!

Books by Darrell and Pamela Hines

The Disease Called 'Comparisonitis'
Let Them Have Dominion
Resolving Conflict in Marriage
A Lifestyle of Healing

To order books or
For ministry information contact:

Christian Faith Fellowship Church
8605 W. Good Hope Road
Milwaukee, WI 53224
(414) 760-2332

www.christianfaithfellowship.org